THE  Best of the B

Norfolk

The need for these guides came to me because I could find no handy single source on British counties, that showed me the things to see and do, the places to stay, eat or drink, that would add zing, interest and variety to my trip.

If you aim to enjoy the best a place can offer, as a weekender, tourer or holidaymaker then you must turn for help to the best-respected, independent authorities. These we have listed on the back cover. We have chosen 17 categories of information, that we believe will have the widest appeal, and succinctly summarized the results for you, with rating marks in six of them.

Now you can choose how to plan your own leisure from a total of over 300 well-researched recommendations for the county of Norfolk.

The map has a grid and every listing in the book has a grid reference as well as a postcode, location information and contacts. Armed with this you can find a listing for any symbol on the map or locate a symbol for any listing in the book.

We believe you are now equipped to get more out of your visit to Norfolk than ever before because the Best of Britain, is simply, the Best there is.

Ross Harvey Publisher

Medieval Priory at Castle Acre

Oyster Mapping Limited

The County of Norfolk

'Norfolk... very flat, Norfolk' is a famous line in Noel Coward's play *Private Lives*. This is not strictly accurate: much of Norfolk undulates, but it is true that the highest point in the county is only 338ft. above sea level, and is the lowest high point among all English counties. It is scarcely higher than the spire of Norwich Cathedral (315ft.). Norfolk is England's fifth largest county, spread over about 2,000 square miles, but its population is a slender 800,000 or so, so there is plenty of peace and quiet to be found.

Norfolk has, for all its long coast line, a very low annual rainfall, which favours visitors, and constant blue skies, so beloved of artists who have always been attracted by its broad land and seascapes. In medieval times, the wool industry brought prosperity to the area, and one of its legacies is remarkably fine architecture. So notable is it that Simon Jenkins has observed the fact that later Georgians and Victorians could never come close to matching it. So they left it alone. **Cawston** and **Salle** (pronounced Saul) in the east and **Walpole St.Peter** in the west are among enthusiasts' favourites.
It was Flemish weavers in the 14th century who gave rise to that prosperity... the town of **Worstead** gave its name (minus the 'a') to a particular weave of woollen cloth. But during the Industrial Revolution the clothmaking industry moved to northern England. However it left behind it many wonderfully preserved old manor houses, often moated, that give the countryside today a special and dignified appeal.

That decline in the manufacturing industry, happily for Norfolk, came just as the Agricultural Revolution was taking hold. Two enlightened and aristocratic landowners during this period were 'Turnip' Townshend of Raynham Hall and Thomas Coke (pronounced 'Cook') of Holkham Hall. They oversaw the replacement of medieval farming methods with crop rotation and the use of manure. Further increasingly efficient farming practices have kept Norfolk to the forefront of today's agricultural industry.

The ever-popular **Norfolk Broads** have National Park status and form the largest protected wetlands area in England, at over 5,000 acres. They are a paradise for both wildlife enthusiasts and families on boating holidays. **King's Lynn**, always worth visiting, welcomes a new marina in 2009 as part of its continuing restoration of the old docks area. A currently popular destination is **Swaffham**, which is the location for the TV series Kingdom.

 **Salhouse Broad**

Some old and great agricultural fortunes have produced two neighbouring Palladian homes of a truly palatial scale. **Houghton** was built by **Sir Robert Walpole**, England's first Prime Minister. Such was its construction cost to him, that debts caused it to pass in the next generation to his great-grandson, the 1st Marquess of Cholmondeley. The more restrained Italianate approach to the creation of **Holkham Hall** by Thomas Coke has equal appeal. **Sandringham**, which The Queen owns personally, looks almost ordinary by comparison, but its immaculately maintained 60 acre garden, within a much larger park, are much admired by its many visitors.

A distinctive feature of Norfolk's landscape is the large number of round church towers; there are about one hundred of them, and are generally beautifully maintained. Some are of Saxon origin but most are Norman, as is **Norwich Cathedral** which dominates the city that grew around it in prosperous times. Visitor trails always include the Castle, old streets, many still lined with ancient dwellings, and **St. Peter Mancroft**. Simon Jenkins has written: 'Few who enter St. Peter's for the first time can stifle a gasp'.

Norfolk possesses two five-star golf courses and two Blue Flag beaches. The Pathfinder series of guidebooks has some interesting walks.
The absence of steep hills and plenty of good pubs indicate good cycling country, and there are also both fine restaurants and accommodation of all standards to be discovered with the help of recommendations in this publication.

Ross Harvey

HOTELS

The Good Hotel Guide 2008 / Alistair Sawday

Children welcome unless marked X, a figure is minimum age - ® ~ best of the rest
No pets unless marked P or (P) restricted - £ ~ B&B per person - (£) ~ B&B per couple

Throughout this guide, the right hand column contains the map grid reference.

Blakeney	**Blakeney Hotel**	Nr Holt, NR25 7NE		G8
	01263 740797	www.blakeney-hotel.co.uk		£77-131
Brancaster Staithe	**The White Horse**	PE31 8BY		D8
	01485 210262	www.whitehorsebrancaster.co.uk	P	£50-75
Burnham Market	**The Hoste Arms**	The Green, PE31 8HD		E8
	01328 738777	www.hostearms.co.uk		(£)122-216
Fritton	**Fritton House**	Church Lane, NR31 9HA		L4
	01493 484008	www.frittonhouse.co.uk	(P)	£70-135
Great Bircham	**The King's Head**	Lynn Rd, PE31 6RJ		D7
	01485 578265	www.the-kings-head-bircham.co.uk		£63-100

▲ Morston Hall

Holt	**Byfords**	1-3 Shirehall Plain, NR25 6BG		G7
	01263 711400	www.byfords.org.uk		£60-95
Holkham	**The Victoria at Holkham**	Park Rd, NR23 1RG		E8
	01328 711008	www.victoriaatholkham.co.uk		£60-130
King's Lynn	**®Kongham Hall**	Lynn Rd, Grimstone, PE32 1AH		D5
	01485 600250	www.konghamhallhotel.co.uk		£80-183
Morston	**Morston Hall**	Morston Holt, NR25 7AA		G8
	01262 741041	www.morstonhall.com	(P)	£140-160
North Walsham	**Beachwood**	Cromer Rd, NR28 0HD		J7
	01692 403231	www.beachwood-hotel.co.uk	10	£45-80
Norwich	**By Appointment**	25-29 St George's St, NR3 1AD		J4
	01603 630730	www.byappointmentnorwich.co.uk	12	£55-85
	®Annesley House	6 Newmarket Rd, NR2 2LA		J4
	01603 624553	www.bw-annesleyhouse.co.uk		£42-118
	®Barnham Broom Hotel	Honingham Rd, NR9 4DD		G4
	01603 759393	www.bannham-broom.co.uk		£70-145
	®Beaufort Lodge	62 Earlham Rd, NR2 3DF		J4
	01603 627928	www.beaufortlodge.com		£33-55
	®Catton Old Hall	Lodge Lane, NR6 7HG		J5
	01603 419339	www.catton-hall.co.uk		£35-60
	Norfolk Mead	Church Loke, NR12 7DN		J5
	01603 737531	www.norfolkmead.co.uk		£50-95
Ringstead	**Gin Trap Inn**	High St, PE36 5JU		C7
	01485 525264	www.gintrapinn.co.uk	X	(£)70-120
Snettisham	**The Rose & Crown**	Old Church Rd, PE31 7LX		C7
	01485 541382	www.roseandcrownsnettisham.co.uk		£43-80
Swaffham	**Strattons**	4 Ash Close, PE37 7NH		E4
	01760 723845	www.strattonshotel.com	(P)	£75-175
Thorpe St Andrew	**The Old Rectory**	103 Yarmouth Rd, NR7 0HF		J4
	01603 700772	www.oldrectorynorwich.com	(P)	£58-110
Titchwell	**Titchwell Manor**	Nr Brancaster, PE31 8BB		D8
	01485 210221	www.titchwellmanor.co.uk	(X)	£45-110
Wells-next-the-Sea	**The Globe Inn**	The Buttlands, NR23 1AU		F8
	01328 710206	www.globewells.co.uk		£65-130
Wolterton	**The Saracen's Head**	Nr Erpingham, NR11 7LX		H7
	01263 768909	www.sarasonshead-norfolk.co.uk	(P)	£45-50

BED & BREAKFAST ACCOMODATION 2008

Good B&B Guide / Wolsey Lodges / Alastair Sawday / Britain's Finest / Unique Homestays / Oyster Mapping

Children welcome unless marked X, a figure is minimum age
No pets, unless marked P or (P) restricted

Location	Name	Address	Min Age	Pets	Grid
Aylsham	**The Old Pump House** 01263 733789	2 Holman Road, NR11 6BY www.britainsfinest.com		(P)	H6
Beetley	**Peacock House** 01362 860371	Peacock Lane, NR20 4DG www.smoothhound.co.uk/hotels/peacockh.html			F5
Brockdish	**Grove Thorp** 01379 668305	Grove Rd, IP21 4JR www.grovethorp.co.uk	12		H2
Broome	**Broome Lodge** 01508 518177	Loddon Rd, NR35 2HX www.broomelodge.co.uk	12		K3
Bungay	**Earsham Park Farm** 01986 892180	Old Railway Road, NR35 2AQ www.earsham-parkfarm.co.uk		(P)	K2
Colton	**The Old Rectory** 01603 880382	Church Lane, NR9 5DE www.britainsfinest.com	12		H5
Cromer	**Incleborough House** 01263 515939	Lower Common, East Runton, NR27 9PG www.incleboroughhouse.co.uk		(P)	H8
	Beach Comber 01263 513398	17 McDonald Rd, NR27 6AP www.beachcomber-guesthouse.co.uk	8		J8
	Elwin House 01263 512170	13 Alfred Rd, NR27 9AN			H8
Dereham	**Kesmark House** 01362 637663	Swanton Morley, NR20 4PP www.kesmarkhouse.co.uk		(P)	F5
	Peacock House 01362 860371	Old Beetley, NR20 4DG www.peacock-house.co.uk	6		F5
Diss	**Rushall House** 01379 741557	Dickleburgh Road, Rushall, IP21 4RX www.rushallhouse.co.uk		(P)	H2
	Church Farm House 01379 687270	Church Road, North Lopham, IP22 2LP www.churchfarmhouse.org	14	(P)	G2
Fakenham	**Glebe Farmhouse** 01328 730133	Wells Rd. North Creake, NR21 9LG www.glebe-farmhouse.co.uk			E7
Fakenham	**Highfield Farm** 01328 829249	Great Ryburgh, NR21 7AL www.broadland.com/highfield.html			E6
Fincham	**Rose Cottage** 01366 347426	Downham Rd, PE33 9HF	8	(P)	C4
Great Yarmouth	**Senglea Lodge** 01493 859632	7 Euston Rd, NR30 1DX			M4
Halvergate	**Manor House** 01493 700279	Tunstall, NR13 3PS www.manorhousenorfolk.co.uk		(P)	K4
Happisburgh	**Manor Farmhouse** 01692 651262	NR12 0SA www.northnorfolk.co.uk/manorbarn	7		K6
Harlston	**The Old Rectory** 01986 788408	Alburgh, IP20 0BW www.alburgholdrectory.com			J2
Helhoughton	**Woodfarm House** 01485 528586	Helhoughton, NR21 7BT www.woodfarm-house.com			E6
Hemsby	**Old Station House** 01493 732022	North Rd, NR29 4EZ www.oldstationhousebandb.co.uk	14		L5
Hethel	**The Moat House** 01508 578536	Rectory Lane, NR14 8HD www.britainsfinest.com			J4

Heydon	Stable Cottage	Heydon Hall, NR11 6RE		H6
	01263 587343	www.sawdays.co.uk	(P)	
Holt	Hempstead Hall	From A148 at Holt S, NR25 6TN		G7
	01263 712224	www.broadband.com/hempsteadhall		
Horsey	Old Chapel	Horsey Corner, NR29 4EH		L5
	01493 393498	www.northfolkbedbreakfast.com	12	
Hindringham	The Old Vicarage	Blacksmith's Lane, NR21 0QA		F7
	01328 878223	www.sawdays.co.uk		
King's Lynn	Bagthorpe Hall	Bagthorpe, PE31 6QY		D7
	01485 578528	www.bagthorpehall.co.uk		
	Lower Farm	Harpley, PE31 6TU		D7
	01485 520240	www.sawdays.co.uk	12 (P)	
	Manor House Farm	Wellingham, Fakenham, PE32 2TH		E5
	01328 838227	www.manor-house-farm.co.uk	10	
	Litcham Hall	Litcham, PE32 2QQ		E5
	01328 701389	www.sawdays.co.uk	(P)	
Long Stratton	Le Grys Barn	Wacton Common, NR15 2UR		H3
	01508 531576	www.legrys-barn.co.uk		
Melton Constable	Burgh Parva Hall	NR24 2PU		G7
	01263 862569	www.sawdays.co.uk		
Melton Constable	Stody Hall	NR24 2ED		G7
	01263 860549	www.stodyhall.co.uk	12 (P)	
Norwich	The Buttery	Berry Hall, Honingham, NR9 5AX		H5
	01603 880541	www.sawdays.co.uk		
	Washingford House	Cookes Road, Bergh Apton, NR15 1AA		J3
	01508 550924	www.sawdays.co.uk	12	
	Sloley Hall	NR12 8HA		K5
	01692 538582	www.sloleyhall.com		
	Arbor Linden Lodge	557 Earlham Rd, NR4 7HW		H4
	01603 451303	www.guesthousenorwich.com		
Ridlington	The Old Rectory	NR28 9NZ		J6
	01692 650247	www.oldrectory.northnorfolk.co.uk		
Saxlingham	Map House	Smokers Hole, NR25 7JU		G8
	01263 741304	www.maphouse.net	X P	
Saxlingham Thorpe	Foxhole Farm	Windy Lane, NR15 1UG		J3
	01508 499226		14	
Sheringham	Fairlawns	26 Hooks Hill Rd, NR26 8NL		H8
	01263 824717			
South Lopham	Oxfootstone Granary	Low Comman, IP22 2JS		G2
	01379 687490	www.oxfoot.co.uk	5 P	
Sporle	Corfield House	0.5m North A47, 3m E of Swaffham, PE32 2EA		E5
	01760 723636	www.corfieldhouse.co.uk	(P)	
Snetterton	Holly House	Snetterton South End, NR16 2LG		G2
	01953 498051	www.hollyhouse-guesthouse.co.uk	12	
Stoke Ferry	Ashpond House	Oxbough Rd, PE33 9TA		C4
	01366 500447	www.ashpondhouse.co.uk		
Thetford	College Farm	Thompson, Thetford, IP24 1QG		E2
	01953 483318	www.sawdays.co.uk	7	
	White Hall	Carbrooke, nr. Watton, IP25 6SG		E4
	01953 885950	www.britainsfinest.com	(P)	
Thompson	Thatched House	IP24 1PH		E2
	01953 483577		6 (P)	
Thursford Green	Holly Lodge	NR21 0AS		F7
	01328 878465	www.hollylodgeguesthouse.co.uk		

8 Bed & Breakfast / Pubs

Tuttington	**Tuttington Hall**	NR11 6TL		H6
	01263 733417	www.wolseylodges.com	(P)	
Walcott	**Holly Tree Cottage**	Walcott Green, NR12 0NS		K6
	01692 650721	www.theaa.com/hotels/102868.html	X	
Waterden	**Old Rectory**	Off B1355 4m NW of Fakenham, NR22 6AT		F7
	01328 823298		P	
Wellingham	**Manor House Farm**	PE32 2TH		E5
	01328 838227		10 (P)	
Wells-next-the-Sea	**Fern Cottage**	Standard Road, NR23 1JU		F8
	01328 710306	www.ferncottage.co.uk		
	The Normans	1 Invaders Court, Standard Rd, NR23 1JW		F8
	01328 710657		14	
Winterton-on-Sea	**Tower Cottage**	Black St, NR29 4AP		L5
	01493 394053	www.towercottage.co.uk	12	
Wymondham	**Sallowfield Cottage**	Wattlefield, NR18 9PA		G3
	01953 605086	www.sallowfieldcottage.co.uk	9 (P)	

PUBS

The Good Pub Guide 2008

D ~ Dining - B ~ Beds - +/++ ~ outstanding - ® ~ Best of the Rest
dogs allowed in bar unless marked ∫ - children allowed in eating areas unless marked X

Bawburgh	**Kings Head**	Harts Lane off B1108, NR9 3LS		H4
	01603 744977		D	
Blakeney	**Kings Arms**	West Gate Street, NR25 7NQ		G8
	01263 740341			
	White Horse	Off A149 W of Sheringham, NR25 7AL		G8
	01263 740574			
Brancaster Staithe	**Jolly Sailors**	Main Road A149, PE31 8BJ		E7
	01485 210314			
	White Horse	A149 E of Hunstanton, PE31 8BY		E7
	01485 210262		BD	
Burnham Market	**Hoste Arms**	The Green, (B1155), PE31 8HD		E8
	01328 738777	*Dining Pub of the Year*	BD	
Burnham Thorpe	**Lord Nelson**	Nr Burnham Market, PE31 8HL		E7
	01328 738241			
Cley-next-the-Sea	**®George**	High Street, NR25 7RN		G8
	01263 740652			
Colkirk	**Crown**	Off B1146 S of Fakenham, NR21 7AA		F6
	01328 862172			
Coltishall	**®Kings Head**	26 Wroxham Road, NR12 7EA		J5
	01603 266113			
Erpingham	**Saracens Head**	Calthorpe/Wolterton, NR11 7LZ		H7
	01263 768909		BD	
Holkham	**Victoria**	A149 nr Holkham Hall, NR23 1RG		F8
	01328 711008		B	
Itteringham	**Walpole Arms**	Off B1354, NR11 7AR		H7
	01236 587258		D	
Larling	**Angel**	Off B1111, NR16 2QU		G2
	01953 717963		B	
Morston	**Anchor**	The Street, NR25 7AA		G8
	01263 741392			

▲ Hoste Arms Hotel, Burnham Market

Norwich	Adam & Eve	Bishopgate, NR3 1RZ		J4
	01603 667423			
	Fat Cat	West End Street, NR2 4NA		J4
	01603 624364			
Old Buckenham	Gamekeeper	The Green, NR17 1RE		G3
	01953 860397			
Ringstead	Gin Trap	Nr Hunstanton, PE36 5JU		C7
	01485 525264		D	
Snettisham	Rose & Crown	N of Sandringham, PE31 7LX		C7
	01485 541382		BD	
South Creake	Ostrich	Burnham Market/Fakenham, NR21 9PB		E7
	01328 823320			
Stanhoe	Crown	B1155, PE31 8QD		E7
	01485 518330			
Stiffkey	Red Lion	A149 Wells-Blakeney, NR23 1AJ		F8
	01328 830552			

10 Pubs

Stoke Holy Cross	®Wildebeest Arms 01508 492497	82/86 Norwich Road, NR14 8QJ	J4
Stow Bardolf	Hare Arms 01366 382229	N of Downham Market, PE34 3HT	C4
Swanton Morley	Darbys 01362 637647	B1147 NE of Dereham, NR20 4NY	G5
Terrington St John	Woolpack 01945 881097	W of King's Lynn, PE14 7RR	A5
Thornham	Lifeboat 01485 512236	Off A149, PE36 6LT	C8 B
Tivetshall St Mary	Old Ram 01379 676794	A140 15m S of Norwich, NR15 2DE	H3 B
Warham	Three Horseshoes 01328 710547	NR23 1NL	F8 B +
Wells-next-the-Sea	Crown 01328 710209	The Buttlands, NR23 1EX	F8 B
	Globe 01328 710206	The Buttlands, NR23 1EU	F8
West Beckham	Wheatsheaf 01263 822110	Church Road, NR25 6NX	G7
Winterton-on-Sea	Fishermans Return 01493 393305	The Lane, NR29 4BN	L5 B
Woodbastwick	Fur & Feather 01603 720003	Off B1140 E of Norwich, NR13 6HQ	K5

▲ Fountains of Holkham Hall

Courtesy of Holkham Estate & Bob Farndon

RESTAURANTS
The Good Food Guide 2008
Cooking Marks out of 10 - M ~ One Michelin Star - ® ~ Best of the Rest

Blakeney	Whitehorse Hotel 01263 740574	4 High Street, NR25 7AL www.blakeneywhitehorse.co.uk		G8
Brancaster Staithe	Whitehorse 01485 210262	Main Road, PE31 8BW www.whitehorsebrancaster.co.uk	3	D8
Brundall	Lavender House 01603 712215	39 The High Street, NR13 5AA www.thelavenderhouse.co.uk	2	J4
Burnham Deepdale	®Deepdale Café 01485 211055	Main Road, PE31 8DD www.deepdalecafe.co.uk		E7
Burnham Market	Fishes 01328 738588	Market Place, PE31 8HE www.fishesrestaurant.co.uk	4	E7
	Hoste Arms 01328 738777	The Green, PE31 8HD www.hostearms.co.uk	2	E8
Grimston	Congham Hall, Orangery 01485 600250	Lynn Road, PE32 1AH www.conghamhallhotel.co.uk	4	D6
Harleston	Momiji Japanese Resto 01379 852243	3 Redenhall Road, IP20 9EN www.momiji-japanese-restaurant.co.uk	2	J2
Holkham	Victoria 01328 711008	Park Road, NR23 1RG www.victoriaatholkham.co.uk	3	F8
Holt	®Cookies Crab Shop 01263 740352	The Green, Salthouse, NR25 7AJ		G8
	®The Three Pigs 01263 587634	Norwich Road, Edgefield, NR24 2RL		G7
King's Lynn	Maggie's Restaurant 01553 771483	11 Saturday Market Place, PE30 5DQ www.rococorestaurant.org.uk	3	C5
	®The Dabbling Duck 01485 520827	Great Massingham, PE32 2HN		E5
	®Titchwell Manor 01485 210221	Titchwell, PE31 8BB		D8
Morston	Morston Hall 01263 741041	NR25 7AA www.mortonhall.com	6	G8
Norwich	Mad Moose Arms and 1Up Restaurant 01603 627687	2 Warwick St, NR2 3LD	2	J4
	Tatlers 01603 766670	21 Tombland, NR3 1RF www.tatlers.com	3	J4
	®Delia's Resturant & Bar 01603 218705	Norwich City Football Club, NR1 1JE www.deliascanarycatering.com		J4
	®Mackintosh's Canteen 01603 305280	Unit 410, Chapelfield Plain, NR2 1SZ www.mackintoshscanteen.co.uk		J4
Ovington	Brovey Lair 01953 882706	Carbrooke Road, IP25 6SD www.broveylair.com	5	F4
Snettisham	®Rose and Crown 01485 541382	Old Church Road, PE31 7LX		C7
Stoke Holy Cross	Wildebeest Arms 01508 492497	82-86 Norwich Road, NR14 8QJ	2	J4
Swaffham	Strattons 01760 723845	4 Ash Close, PE37 7NH www.strattonshotel.com	3	E4
Walsingham	Norfolk Riddle Restaurant 01328 821903	2 Wells Road, NR22 6DJ		F7

12 Churches

CHURCHES
England's Thousand Best Churches by Simon Jenkins
Marks out of 5 - nearest postcode quoted

Attleborough	St Mary	On outskirts of town, NR17 2AH	3	G3
Barton Turf	St Michael	Outside village in a grove of trees, NR12 8YU	1	K5
Beeston	St Mary	1m from village on a hillock near a farm, PE32 2LY1		E5
Binham	Priory of St Mary	NR21 0DR	2	F7
Blakeney	St Nicholas	Above the harbour, NR25 7NJ	3	G8
Booton	St Michael	NR10 4NZ	2	H6
Brisley	St Bartholomew	NR20 5AA	1	F6
Burnham Deepdale	St Mary	PE31 8DQ	1	E7
Burnham Norton	St Margaret	PE31 8DW	1	E7
Burnham Overy	St Clement	1m inland from old harbour on hill, PE31 8HX	1	E7
Castle Acre	St James	PE32 2AE	1	E5
Cawston	St Agnes	NR10 4AJ	3	H6

◀ St Peter and St Paul Church, Salle

Churches 13

Cley-next-the-Sea	St Margaret	NR25 7TT	3	G8
Cromer	St Peter and St Paul	NR27 9EY	1	H8
East Dereham	St Nicholas	NR19 2ED	2	F5
East Harling	St Peter and St Paul	NR16 2NA	2	G2
Glandford	St Martin	Down the road from Cley via a ford, NR25 7JR	1	G8
Gooderstone	St George	Centre of village beyond Oxburgh Hall, PE33 9BY	2	D4
Great Walsingham	St Peter	Sits on a knoll outside the village, NR22 6DW	2	F7
Great Yarmouth	St Nicholas	NR30 1NE	3	M4
Haddiscoe	St Mary	On a peninsula formed by the River Waveney S of The Broads, NR14 6PB	1	K3
Hales	St Margaret	1m S of village, NR14 6QL	1	K3
Happisburgh	St Mary	NR12 0PN	1	K6
Harpley	St Lawrence	On a lane away from the village, PE31 6TN	1	D6
Heydon	St Peter and St Paul	NR11 6AD	1	H6
Hingham	St Andrew	NR9 4HP	2	G4
King's Lynn	St Margaret	PE30 5DU	4	C5
King's Lynn	St Nicholas	PE30 1QS	1	C5
Knapton	St Peter and St Paul	NR28 0AD	1	J7
Little Snoring	St Andrew	On slope over the stream, NR21 0HT	1	F7
Ludham	St Catherine	NR29 5AB	2	K6
Merton	St Peter	In Merton Hall park land, IP25 6QH	1	F4
Mundford	St Leonard	In the outskirts of village, IP26 5DN	1	D3
North Creake	St Mary	On the Burnham Rd, NR21 9JJ	1	E7
North Elmham	St Mary	NR20 5JU	1	F6
North Walsham	St Nicholas	Behind houses, above market place, NR28 9BT	1	J6
Northwold	St Andrew	IP26 5NE	2	D3
Norwich	Octagon Chapel	Colegate, NR3 1BN	2	J4
Norwich	St Andrew	St Andrews St, NR3 1AU	1	J4
Norwich	St Peter Mancroft	Market Place, NR2 1RD	4	J4
Outwell	St Clement	PE14 8PZ	1	B4
Oxborough	St John	PE33 9PS	2	D4
Pulham	St Mary	IP21 4RD	2	H2
Ranworth	St Helen	NR13 6HS	3	K5
Salle	St Peter and St Paul	NR10 4SF	4	H6
Salthouse	St Nicholas	NR25 7XQ	2	G8
Shelton	St Mary	NR15 2SD	2	H3
Snettisham	St Mary	PE31 7LA	2	C7
South Creake	St Mary	NR21 9LX	1	E7
South Lopham	St Andrew	IP22 2LW	2	G2
Stow Bardolph	Holy Trinity	PE34 3HT	1	C5
Swaffham	St Peter and St Paul	PE37 7QN	2	E4
Terrington	St Clement	PE34 4LZ	3	B5
Thorpe Market	St Margaret	NR11 8AJ	1	J7
Thurning	St Andrew	NR20 5QX	1	F6
Tilney	All Saints	W of King's Lynn, PE34 4SW	2	B5
Tittleshall	St Mary	On outskirts of village, PE32 2PN	1	E5
Trunch	St Botolph	NR28 0PZ	2	J7
Upwell	St Peter	PE14 9AA	2	A4
Walpole	St Peter	PE14 7NS	5	A5
West Walton	St Mary	PE14 7ET	3	A5
Wiggenhall	St Germans	PE34 3EU	2	B5
Wiggenhall	St Mary Magdalen	Middle of the village, PE34 3DG	2	B5
Worstead	St Mary	NR28 9AL	3	J6
Wymondham	The Abbey	NR18 9PH	3	G3

HOUSES

England's Thousand Best Houses by Simon Jenkins

Marks out of 5 - NT ~ National Trust - EH ~ English Heritage - P ~ Private - R ~ Restricted
M ~ Museum - H ~ Hotel

Blickling Hall	1.5m NW of Aylsham, NR11 6NF	01263 738030	4	NT	H6
Castle Acre Priory	4m N of Swaffham, PE32 2XD	01760 755394	2	EH	E5
The Castle	Castle Rising, NE of King's Lynn, PE31 6AH	01553 631330	2	EH	D7
Trinity Hospital	Castle Rising, NE of King's Lynn, PE31 6AG		1	P/R	C6
Iceni House	Cockley Cley, 4m SW of Swaffham, PE37 8AN		1	M	E4
Old Cottage	Cockley Cley, 4m SW of Swaffham, PE37 8AN		1	M	D4
Fisherman's Cottage	Cromer Museum, NR27 9HB	01263 513543	1	M	H8
Felbrigg Hall	2m SW of Cromer, NR11 8PR	01263 837444	3	NT	J7
Elizabethan House	4 South Quay, Gt. Yarmouth, NR30 2QH	01493 855746	2	M	M4
Row Houses	Gt. Yarmouth, NR30 2RG	01493 857900		EH	M4
Row 111	South Quay, Gt. Yarmouth, NR30 2RG	01493 857 900	1		M4
Row 113	South Quay, Gt. Yarmouth, NR30 2RG		1		M4
Holkham Hall	2m W of Wells-next-the-sea, NR23 1AB	01328 710227	5	P	F8
Houghton Hall	10m W of Fakenham, PE31 6UE	01485 528569	4	P	D7
Clifton House	17 Queen St, King's Lynn, PE30 1HU		2	P	C6
Old Gaol House	Saturday Market, King's Lynn, PE30 5DQ	01553 774297	1	M	C5
Mannington House	7m SE of Holt, NR11 7BB	01263 584175	2	P/R	H7
Norwich Castle	Castle Meadow, Norwich, NR1 3JU	01603 493625	1	M	J4
Dragon Hall	115-23 King St, Norwich, NR1 1QE	01603 663922	1	M	J4
Strangers' Hall	Charing Cross, Norwich, NR2 4AL	01603 667229	2	M	J4
Oxburgh Hall	7m SW of Swaffham, PE33 9PS	01366 328258	4	NT	C4
Sandringham House	8m NE of King's Lynn, PE35 6EN	01553 612908	3	P	C6
Old Hall	South Burlingham, E of Norwich, NR13 4EY	01493 750804	2	P-R	K4
Ancient House	White Hart St, Thetford, IP24 1AA	01842 752599	1	M	E2
House of Correction	Walsingham, 5m N of Fakenham, NR22 6EA	01328 820259	1	M	F7
Wolterton Hall	4m N of Aylsham, NR11 7BB	01263 584175	2	P	H7

◀ Felbrigg Hall

◀ The Gardens at Houghton House

GARDENS
The Good Gardens Guide 2007 (Peter King / Saga)
To appear in this guide means it is worth a visit
1 ~ superior merit · 2 ~ world class · NT ~ National Trust

Besthorpe Hall	Attleborough, 14m SW Norwich, NR17 2LJ	01953 450300	1	G3
Blickling Hall	15m N of Norwich, NR11 6NF	01263 738030	1 NT	H6
Bradenham Hall	8m E of Swaffham, IP25 7QP	01362 687243	1	F4
Bressingham Gardens	Diss, IP22 2AB	01379 686900	1	G2
Corpusty Mill Garden	Off B1149 6m S of Holt, NR11 6QB	01263 587223	1	H7
Courtyard Farm	116m NE of King's Lynn, PE36 5LQ	01485 525251	1	C7
East Ruston Old Vicarage	15m NE of Norwich, NR12 9HN	01692 650432	2	K6
The Exotic Garden	6 Cotman Road, Thorpe, NR1 4AF	01603 623167		J4
Fairhaven Woodland Water Garden	School Road, South Walsham, NR13 6EA	01603 270449	1	K5
	Norwich, NR13 6DZ	01603 270683		K5
Felbrigg Hall	2m SW of Cromer off A148, NR11 8PR	01263 837444	1 NT	J7
Hales Hall	12m SE of Norwich, NR14 6QW	01508 548507		K3
Holkham Hall	2m W of Wells on A149, NR23 1AB	01328 710227	1	F8
Houghton Hall	13m NE of King's Lynn off A148, PE31 6UE	01485 528569	2	D7
Hoveton Hall Gardens	1m N of Wroxham on A1151, NR12 8RJ	01603 782798		J5
How Hill Farm	15m NE Norwich, NR29 5PG	01692 678558	1	K5
Kettle Hill	By Blakeney on B1156, NR25 7PN	01263 741147	1	G8
Lawn Farm	Cley Road, Holt, NR25 7DY	01263 713484		G8
Lexham Hall	6m N of Swaffham, PE32 2QJ	01328 701288		E5
Mannington Hall	5m SE of Holt off B1149, NR11 7BB	01263 584175	1	H7
Oxburgh Hall	7m SW of Swaffham off A134, PE33 9PS	01366 328258	NT	C4
Pensthorpe	1m E of Fakenham, NR21 0LN	01328 851465	1	F6
Sandringham House	9m W of King's Lynn on B1440, PE35 6EN	01553 772675	1	C6
Sheringham Park	4m NE of Holt off A148, NR26 8TL	01263 820550	1 NT	H8
Stow Hall	2m N of Downham Market, PE34 3HU	01366 383194	1	C5
Wretham Lodge	6m NE of Thetford off A1075, IP24 1RL	01953 498997		E2

BEACHES

⚜ ~ Recommended by Marine Conservation Society For Top Water Quality Rating 2008

⚑ ~ a full range of amenities, including lifeguards

Beaches listed anticlockwise

Wells-next-the-Sea	Wells	E8	**Great Yarmouth**	Great Yarmouth Pier	
Norwich	Sea Palling	L6		(Marina Leisure centre)	M4
Mundesley	Mundesley ⚑	K7		Great Yarmouth North	M5
Winterton-on-Sea	Hemsby ⚑	M5		Caister Point	M5
Kings Lynn	Heacham - S.Sands Club	C7	**Cromer**	Cromer ⚑	J8

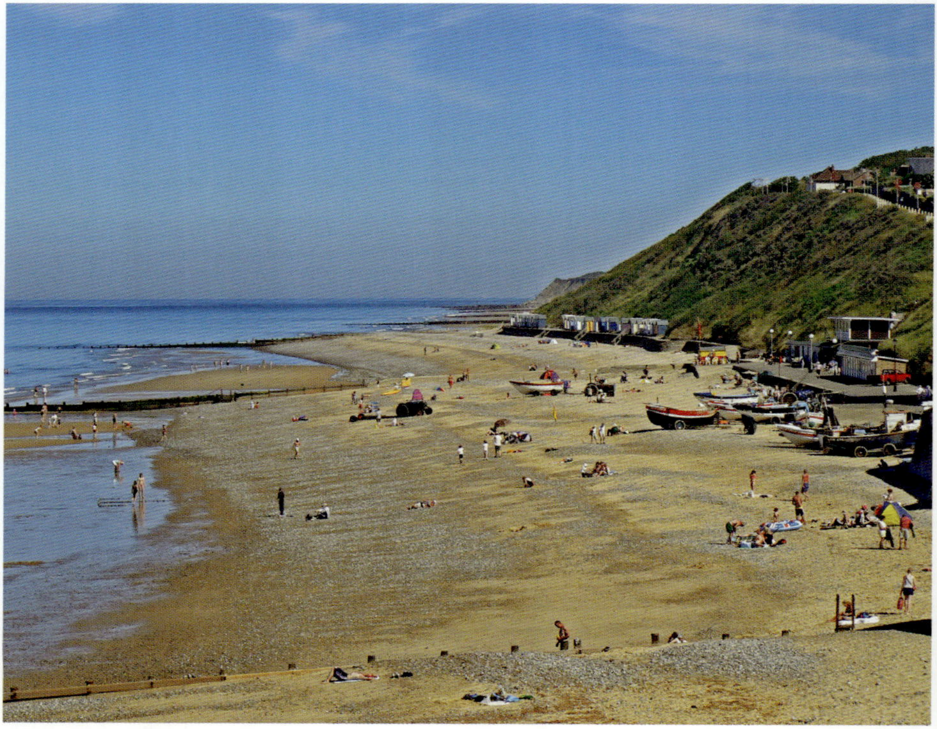

▲ **Cromer Beach, Norfolk**

Outstanding Views / Archaeologoy **17**

OUTSTANDING VIEWS
Oyster Mapping
Nearest postcode quoted

Beacon Hill   338 Feet, highest point in the county, West Runton, NR27 9ND   H8

 Salhouse Moorings

ARCHAEOLOGY
Oyster Mapping
Nearest postcode quoted

Burgh Castle	In places the Roman walls still stand to their full height Great Yarmouth, NR31 9QJ	L4
Caistor St Edmund	Roman Town, Norwich, NR14 8RH	J4
Tasburgh Fort	Likely to be Iron Age (just before the Roman period), but its date is unproven Long Stratton, NR15 1NH	J3
Binham Priory	A ruined Benedictine priory, Fakenham, NR21 0DQ	F7
St Benets Abbey	Drainage mill, possibly originally built to crush cole seed to make colza oil Horning, NR29 5NU	K5
Bloodgate Hill Fort	Iron Age Hill Fort, South Creake, NR21 9LZ	E7
Site of Unitarian Chapel	Filby, NR29 3HJ	L5
Middleton Mount	Motte and bailey earthwork, constructed by the Normans about 1200 Middleton, PE32 1YB	D5
Woodcock Hall	Iron Age to Roman settlement and Roman forts, Watton, IP25 7AB	F4
Caister Castle	Late Roman 'Saxon Shore' fort and Middle to Late Saxon cemetery Caister on Sea, NR30 5SN	

18 Museums & Galleries

MUSEUMS & GALLERIES
Britain's Best Museums & Galleries by Mark Fisher
Marks out of 5

Houghton House	King's Lynn, PE31 6UE	3	D6
www.houghtonhall.com	01485 528569		
Norwich Castle Museum	Norwich, NR1 3JU	3	J4
www.norfolk.gov.uk	01603 493625		
Sainsbury Centre for Visual Arts	University of East Anglia, Norwich, NR4 7TJ	3	H4
www.uea.ac.uk/scva	01603 593199		
Holkham Hall	Wells-next-the-Sea, NR23 1AB	3	F8
www.holkham.co.uk	01328 710227		

▲ **Norwich Castle Museum**

FAMILY ATTRACTIONS
Oyster Mapping

Aylsham	**Bure Valley Railway** - Steam trains and Broads Cruise		H6
	Norwich Road, NR11 6BW	01263 733858	www.bvrw.co.uk
Bircham	**Bircham Windmill** - Fully restored windmill with onsite bakery and visitors tour.		D7
	Kings Lynn, PE31 6SJ	01485 578393	www.birchamwindmill.co.uk
Castle Acre	**Castle Acre Priory** - Perhaps the finest example of Norman estate planning		E5
	Stocks Green, PE32 2XD	01760 755394	www.english-heritage.org.uk
Diss	**Bressingham Steam and Gardens** - 3 Steam Hauled trains		G2
	High Road, IP22 2AB	01379 686900	www.bressingham.co.uk
Downham Market	**Collectors World** - Nelson, Barbara Cartland, Car Museum, Wildlife Santuary		B4
	Black Drove, PE38 0AU	01366 383185	www.collectors-world.org
Fakenham	**Langham Glass Ltd** - Watch Master glass makers at work		E6
	Sculthorpe Boulevard, NR21 7RL	01485 529111	www.langhamglass.co.uk
	Pensthorpe Nature Reserve and Gardens - Hosting BBC Springwatch 2008		F6
	Fakenham Road, NR21 0LN	01328 851465	www.pensthorpe.com
	The Thursford Collection - Fairground, Musical organs		F7
	High Street, NR21 0AS	01328 878 477	www.thursford.com
Filby	**Thrigby Wildlife Gardens** - Renowned collection of Asian mammals, birds and reptiles		L5
	Great Yarmouth, NR29 3DR	01493 369477	www.thrigby.plus.com
Gooderstone	**Gooderstone Water Gardens** - 6 acres of garden, ponds, nature trail. Tearoom and shop		D4
	The Street, PE33 9BP	01603 712913	www.gooderstonewatergardens.co.uk
Great Yarmouth	**Fritton Lake** - Wide variety of entertainments set in mature woodland along the banks		L4
	Beccles Road, NR31 9HA	01493 488288	www.somerleyton.co.uk
	Caister Castle Car Collection - An impressive collection of vehicles from 1893 onwards		M4
	Castle Lane, NR30 5SN	01572 787251	www.greateryarmouth.co.uk
Holt	**Muckleburgh Collection** - The UK's largest privately owned working Military Collection		G8
	Weybourne Camp, NR25 7EG	01263 588210	www.muckleburgh.co.uk
Hoveton	**BeWILDerwood** - A huge forest adventure and the Norfolk Broads Cycling Centre.		K5
	Horning Road, NR12 8JW	01603 783900	www.bewilderwood.co.uk
Hunstanton	**Hunstanton Sea Life Sanctuary** - Ocean Tunnel, Sharks, Rays, Seals and Otters		C8
	Southern Promenade, PE36 5BH	01485 533576	www.sealsanctuary.co.uk/hunt1.html
	Norfolk Lavender - "England's Premier Lavender Farm", tours take place regularly		C7
	Caley Mill, PE31 7JE	01485 570384	www.norfolk-lavender.co.uk
	Searles Sea Tours - Five tours available. A fascinating way of discovering The Wash		C7
	South Beach Road, PE36 5BB	01485 534444	www.seatours.co.uk
King's Lynn	**Lynn Museum** - The West Norfolk Story. Lots of activities for all the family		C6
	Market Street, PE30 1NL	01553 775001	www.museums.norfolk.gov.uk
	The Green Quay - Educational Centre about The Wash and surroundings		C5
	Marriotts Warehouse, PE30 5DT	01553 818500	www.thegreenquay.co.uk
	Kings Lynn Town Guides - Nine hundred years of maritime trading history		C6
	Saturday Market Place, PE30 1LT	01553 774297	
Lenwade	**The Big Dinosaur Adventure** - A great fovourite amongst under 10's		H5
	Weston Park, NR9 5JW	01603 876310	www.dinosauradventure.co.uk
Long Sutton	**Butterfly and Wildlife Park** - A unique day out, with hundreds of exotic butterflies		A6
	Spalding, PE12 9LE	01406 363833	www.butterflyandwildlifepark.co.uk
Lowestoft	**Pleasurewood Hills** - Adventure park, with many rides for all the family		M3
	Leisure Way, Corton, NR32 5DZ	01502 586000	www.pleasurewoodhills.com
Lynford	**Thetford Forest** - A century old and very big		E2
	Mark Lane, IP27 0TP		www.forestry.gov.uk/thetfordforestpark

20 Family Attractions

Narborough	**Narborough Trout & Coarse Lakes** - 27 acres of lakes & water meadow in the Nar valley			D5
	Main Road, PE32 1TE	01760 338005	www.narfish.co.uk	
North Pickenham	**Anglia Karting Centre** - 1030 metre floodlit outdoor circuit. For 4ft 4+ and 8yrs up			E4
	Swaffham, PE37 8LL	01760 441777	www.anglia-karting.co.uk	
Norwich	**Banham Zoo** - Over 1000 animals in 35 acres of parkland			G2
	The Grove, NR16 2HE	01953 887771	www.banhamzoo.co.uk	
	City Of Norwich Aviation Museum - Preserving the history of aviation in Norfolk			J5
	Old Norwich Road, NR10 3JF	01603 893080	www.cnam.co.uk	
Reedham	**Pettitts Animal Adventure Park** - Reptile House, Roller Coaster. Covered play area.			L4
	Church Road, NR13 3UA	01493 700094	www.pettittsadventurepark.co.uk	
Sheringham	**The North Norfolk Railway** - 5 Miles, lovely coastal scenery.			H8
	Station Approach, NR26 8RA	01263 820800	www.nnrailway.co.uk	
Snettisham	**Snettisham Park** - Deer safari, trails, farm animals, tractor rides, stables, tea room			C9
	Park Farm, PE31 7NQ	01485 542425	www.snettishampark.co.uk	
Stow Bardolph	**Church Farm** - Rare breeds Centre, nature walks and magnificent gardens			C5
	Lynn Road, PE34 3HT	01366 382162	www.churchfarmstowbardolph.co.uk	
Swaffham	**EcoTech Centre** - Environmental visitor attraction with a café, shop and organic garden			E4
	Turbine Way, PE37 7HT	01760 726100	www.ecotech.org.uk	
Weasenham	**Extreme Adventure** - Adrenalin rushing fun for all the family over 10 years of age			E5
	High House, PE32 2SP	01328 838720	www.extremeadventure.co.uk	
Wells-Next-the-Sea	**Wells and Walsingham Light Railway** - Worlds longest 10¼ inch gauge railway.			F8
	Stiffkey Road, NR23 1QB	01328 711530	www.wellswalsinghamrailway.co.uk	
Welney	**WWT Wetland Centre** - An important nature reserve. With an eco-friendly visitor.			A3
	Hundred Foot Bank, PE14 9TN	01353 860711	www.wwt.org.uk	

◀ **The Stone Hall at Houghton House**

©Houghton House, Norfolk.

NATURAL PRODUCE
Oyster Mapping

Blakeney	**Blakeney Delicatessen** - Cheeses, cooked meats, organic chocolate, olives oils and a selection of wines 01263 740939 NR25 7AL www.blakeneydeli.co.uk	G8
Blofield	**HFG Farm Shop** - Home reared Angus beef, free range pork, fruit, veg and flour 01603 715232 NR13 4LQ www.h-f-g.co.uk	K4
Brooke	**The Booja-Booja Company** - Winner of best organic product 2007, 100% organic chocolate and ice cream 01508 558888 NR15 1HJ www.boojabooja.com	J3
Burnham Market	**Satchells** - Independent, good quality, old fashioned wine shop, stocking over 1200 types of wine 01328 738272 PE31 8HG www.satchellswines.com	E7
Cawston	**Broadland Wines** - Organic fruit and country wines 01603 872474 NR10 4GB www.broadland-wineries.com	H6
Cley-next-the-Sea	**Picnic Fayre** - Friendly shop with daily tastings available of the local products 01263 740587 NR25 7AP www.picnic-fayre.co.uk	G8
Diss	**Goodies Farm Shop** - Described locally as a mini Fortum & Mason, huge range of products, not just local 01379 676880 IP21 4XU www.goodiesfarmshop.co.uk	H2
Fakenham	**J & D Papworth Farms** - Sells through local butchers or bulk order for next day delivery 01328 855039 NR21 9AP www.papworthbutchers.co.uk	F6
Flitcham	**Abbey Farm Organics** - More than 50 organic crops, has a box scheme or single orders 01485 609094 PE31 6BT www.abbeyfarm.co.uk	D6
Hilgay	**Dent's of Hilgay** - Norfolk Broadland wine & Elgood beer, Aberdeen Angus beef and local cheese 01366 385661 PE38 0QH www.dentsofhilgay.com	C3
Holt	**Bakers and Larners** - Traditional dept. store, with a food hall offering a huge selection 01263 712323 NR25 6BW www.bakersandlarners.com	G7
	The North Norfolk Fish Company - Home-made specialities include taramasalata made with cod roe 01263 711913 NR25 6BN	G7
Hunstanton	**Courtyard Farm** - Organic, rare breed beef, lamb and pork. 01485 525251 PE36 5LQ	C7
Kings Lynn	**Groom's Bakery** - Range of traditional breads and some excellent continental breads 01328 738289 PE31 8HD	E7
Letheringsett	**Letheringsett Watermill** - Award winning water mill, stocks 17 types of flour 01263 713153 NR25 7YD www.letheringsettwatermill.co.uk	G8
Melton Constable	**HV Graves** - Local lamb, chickens, and free range beef and pork. 01263 860333 NR24 2LE	G7
	M & M Rutland - Traditional family butcher, selling local free range meats, specialties homemade haggis 01263 860562 NR24 2DG www.rutland-butchers.co.uk	G7
North Walsham	**Tavern Tasty Meats** - Accredited rare breeds butcher, specialising in sausages and pork pies 01692 405444 NR28 0RQ www.taverntasty.co.uk	J7
Reepham	**Diane's Pantry** - Health food & supplements, small organic bakery, local pork pies 01603 871075 NR10 4JJ	H6
Thuxton	**Peeles' Norfolk Black Turkeys** - Producing only naturally reared Norfolk Black turkeys 01362 850237 NR9 4QJ	G4
Wells-next-the-sea	**The Real Ale Shop** - Sells over 50 ales made in Norfolk 01328 710810 NR23 1SB www.therealaleshop.co.uk	F8

▲ A Norfolk Country Lane in Spring

ANTIQUE DEALERS
Oyster Mapping

Coltishall	**Village Clocks** 01603 736047	9 High Street, NR12 7AA	J5
Cromer	**Bond Street Antiques** 01263 513134	6 Bond Street, NR27 9DA	H8
Diss	**Antique & Collectors Centre** 01379 644472	3 Cobbs Yard, St Nicholas Street, IP22 4LB	H2
Earsham	**Mathew Higham Antiques** 01986 896655	3 Park Farm, NR35 2AQ www.matthewhighamantiques.co.uk	K3
Fakenham	**Norfolk Decorative Antiques** 01328 856333	Fakenham Industrial Estate, NR21 8NW www.norfolkdecorativeantiques.co.uk	F6
	Steward David 01328 853535	8 Norwich Road, NR21 8AX	F6
	Fakenham Antique Centre 01328 862341	14 Norwich Road, NR21 8AZ	F7
Great Yarmouth	**Times Past Antiques** 01692 670898	Station Road, Potter Heigham, NR29 5AD	K5
	Howkins Peter 01493 851180	132 King Street, NR30 2PQ	M4
Hales	**MD Cannell Antiques** 01508 548406	The Raveningham Centre, Beccles Road, NR14 6NU	K3
Hingham	**Anglian Antiques** 01953 851749	The Old Barn, Watton Road, NR9 4NN	G4
Holt	**Heathfield Antiques** 01263 711609	Candlestick Lane, Thornage Rd, NR25 6SU www.antique-pine.net	G7
	Mews Antique Emporium 01263 713224	17b High Street, NR25 6BN	G7

Antique Dealers

	Anthony Fell Antiques & Works of Art Ltd 01263 712912	Chester House, 47 Bull Street, NR25 6HP www.anthonyfell.com	G7
Hunstanton	Hunstanton Antiques & Collectables 01485 535554	34 Greevegate, PE36 6AG	C8
King's Lynn	Old Granary Antiques Centre 01553 775509	King Staithe Lane, PE30 1LZ	C6
	Knight R D 01553 775297	75 Gayton Road, PE30 4EH	C5
	Farmhouse Antiques 01366 500588	Whites Farm Hse, Oxborough Rd, PE33 9TA	C4
	Country Antiques 01328 730569	Creake Road, Burnham Market, PE31 8EA	E7
Norwich	Cottage in the Basement 01603 761906	The Undercroft, 14 Tombland, NR3 1HF	J4
	Tombland Antique Centre 01603 619219	Augustine Steward House, 14 Tombland, NR3 1HF	J4
	Silvermans 01603 464746	17 Hatton Road, NR1 2PT	J4
	Nicolas Fowle Antiques 01603 219964	Websdales Court, Bedford Street, NR2 1AR	J4
	Musker Antiques 01603 617573	6 St Gregorys Alley, NR2 1ER	J4
	Mandell's Gallery 01603 626892	Elm Hill, NR3 1HN	J4
	James Brett Antiques & Works of Art 01603 628171	42 St Giles Street, NR2 1LW	J4
	Elm Hill Antiques 01603 667414	28 Elm Hill, NR3 1HG	J4
	Brett James Ltd 01603 628171	42 St Giles Street, NR2 1LW	J4
	Antiques & Interiors 01603 622695	31-35 Elm Hill, NR3 1HG	J4
	Albrow & Sons 01603 622569	10 All Saints Green, NR1 3NA	J4
Old Hunstanton	Le Strange Old Barns 01485 533402	Golf Course Road, PE36 6JG www.lestrangeoldbarns.co.uk	C8
Raveningham	East India Trading Depot 01508 548406	The Raveningham Centre, Castell Farm, NR14 6NU	K3
Ringstead	Ringstead Village Antique Centre 01485 525270	41 High Street, PE36 5JU	C8
Stalham	William James Antiques & Interiors Ltd 01692 584777	110 High Street, NR12 9AU www.williamjamesantiques.co.uk	K6
Swaffam	Buckie Antiques 01760 721052	59 Market Place, PE37 7LE www.buckie-antiques.com	E4
Thetford	The Antique Shop 01842 755511	8 White Hart Street, IP24 1AD	E2
Wells-Next-The-Sea	Staithe Street Antiques, Curios and Collectables 01553 810193	69 Staithe Street, NR23 1AW	F8
Wroxham	T S C Brooke 01603 782644	The Grange, 57 Norwich Road, NR12 8RX	K5

GOLF COURSES

1000 Best Courses in Britain and Ireland by Golf World
Marks out of 5

Hunstanton Golf Club	Golf Course Rd, Old Hunstanton, PE36 6JQ	01485 532811	5	C8
Barnham Broom Hotel Golf Club (Valley)	Honingham, Barnham Broom, Norwich, NR9 4DD	01603 759393	1	G4
Bawburgh Golf Club	Glen Lodge, Marlingford Rd, NR9 3LU	01603 740404	1	H4
Eaton Golf Club	Newmarket Rd, Norwich, NR4 6SF	01603 451686	3	J4
Gorleston Golf Club	Warren Rd, Gorleston, NR31 6JT	01493 661911	2	M4
Great Yarmouth & Caister Golf Club	Beach House, Caister Golf Club, NR30 5TD	01493 728699	3	M4
King's Lynn Golf Club	Castle Rising, King's Lynn, PE31 6BD	01553 631654	3	C6
The Norfolk Golf & Country Club	Hingham Rd, Reymerston, Norwich, NR9 4QQ	01362 850297	1	G4
Royal Cromer Golf Club	145 Overstrand Rd, Cromer, NR7 0JH	01263 512884	3	J4
Royal Norwich Golf Club	Drayton High Rd, Hellsdon, Norwich, NR6 5AH	01603 429928	3	H5
Royal West Norfolk Golf Club	Beach Rd, Brancaster, PE31 8AX	01485 210087	5	D8
Sheringham Golf Club	Weybourne Rd, Sheringham, NR26 8HG	01263 823488	3	H8
Thetford Golf Club	Brandon Rd, Thetford, IP24 3NE	01842 752169	3	E2
Wensum Valley Golf Club (Valley)	Beech Avenue, Taverham, NR8 6HP	01603 261012	2	H5

Royal West Norfolk Golf Club at Brancaster